DOMESTICATED DEMONS

DOMESTICATED DEMONS

Amba Elieff

With Illustrations by
Gabrielle Elizabeth Scarlett

Originally published in 2023.

Published by Queer Creek Publishing 2026
South Bloomingville, OH

If you are inspired to post images of the pages of this text on social media, please tag @amba.elieff. I would love to witness you on your journey.

ISBN: 978-1-968933-06-7

DEMONS

This collection of poetry was inspired by my demons. The traumas, triggers, insecurities, depression, and anxieties that regularly visit me in life. Sometimes the feelings make sense and sometimes they are irrational. That is what demons do to us, make us irrational sometimes. They haunt and hound us. Trying to make sure you don't forget that they exist. Living on the pain in your mind. The mind is a powerful place for demons. It creates a reality that exists just for them. By writing about them and owning them they lose some of their power. They reside in your silence, writing and talking about them shrinks them and makes them leave. I hope you domesticate your demons too.

ALSO BY AMBA ELIEFF

with illustrations by Gabrielle Scarlett

Maiden, Mother, Crone
2022

Naked & Healing
2024

In The Hills
2025

Voices
2026

available at https://ambapoetry.com

Domesticated demons
we all have them
demons we live with
that we have tamed
like pets
never gone
but no longer fierce
they no longer own us
now more like a child
that has a temper tantrum
we acknowledge it

we breathe
and slowly
it subsides
shrinks
quietly into a corner
silently behaving
til the next time

~ *amba elieff*

CONTENTS

ACKNOWLEDGMENTS

For those who hurt and for those who heal.

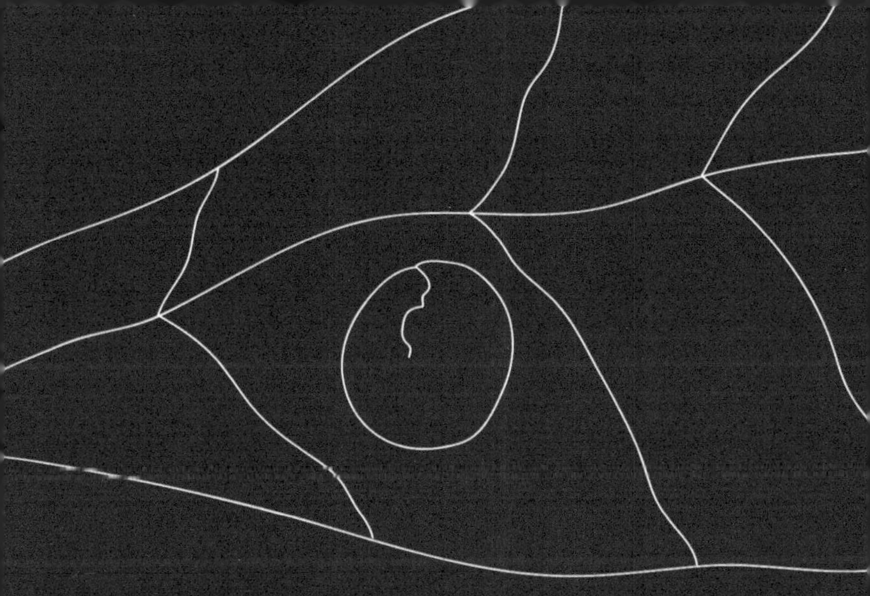

SUMMER SOLSTICE

The longest day of the year. The sun is at its highest elevation. Summer solstice is days before I was born. A younger me, more foolish and naive.

The mornings are the easiest
it is always a new beginning
in the morning
a fresh start
a clean slate
I can believe anything
because nothing has started
I hold you close
like forever
blissfully happy
but as the day wears on
all that morning beginning
clean slate
is smudged and dirty
trust and belief
wears away
and we start over

~ *amba elieff*

He handed me a bouquet
of cliches
love at first sight
not been happy in marriage a long time
staying because he loves his kids
misses me so much he can think of nothing else
has to take care of her
can't stand to be away from me
we are soulmates
like a romance novel
with the sacrifice
to be together
and I believed every word
never seeing the cliches

~ *amba elieff*

When no one listens to you
touches you
sees you
growing up
you search
your entire life
for the one that
will love you
miss you
touch you
hear you
because you have
so many empty holes
and blank spaces
to fill

~ *amba elieff*

My mother gave me my first demons
some of them
I believe
she gave me before birth
given that I was not planned
and
I changed her life
and
I don't think she was happy about it
and she had her own baggage
from before me
that
she stored
inside
in a womb of its own
growing alongside me
twins
she gave birth to me
but the baggage just kept growing

~ *amba elieff*

My first marriage was a suicide
I was trapped in a limo going to a college formal
roses, formal gown, tuxedo
in the back seat, a ring, and the question
my answer
trapped, polite, not willing to say no

"Someday"
someday was out there, somewhere, undefined
and I entered the tunnel
I did not imagine anyone else wanting me
asking me to marry them
wanting to share a life with me
no options
and I saw the other tunnel where I was trapped
in my parents' house
with curfews and disapproval
no way out
so I ended up married
knowing beforehand
I would never be happy

I was trapped in the tunnel
I could see no other options
no other paths
until the day when he was so miserable
because I wasn't what he imagined
that being alone, was better than being with me
and I was right no one else ever asked me
and that is okay

~ *amba elieff*

You never had to lie
I took care of it for you
you never had to answer a question
my mind would
simply
silently
offer up another excuse
another reason
another story
and you never have to feel guilty

~ *amba elieff*

I hope you are never sorry
for taking on the chore of me
the emotions that I can't control
that make me pull away into my shell of a being
anxiety that turns me into knots
fears that are left from the others
fear to be open
fear to believe
fear to speak
the silence where I hide
that you patiently accept
as I work through trying to put together what to
say
what I feel
afraid that speaking my truth will collapse my
fragile world
that you will see me differently
that you will see that I am really a burden
and you will get tired
and walk away
and be done

~ *amba elieff*

He created all my broken pieces
breaking them off one by one
each distortion of reality
each truth uncovered
each subtle lie
and he put them in a box
and handed it to me
and said
find someone who can put that back together
then he walked away

~ *amba elieff*

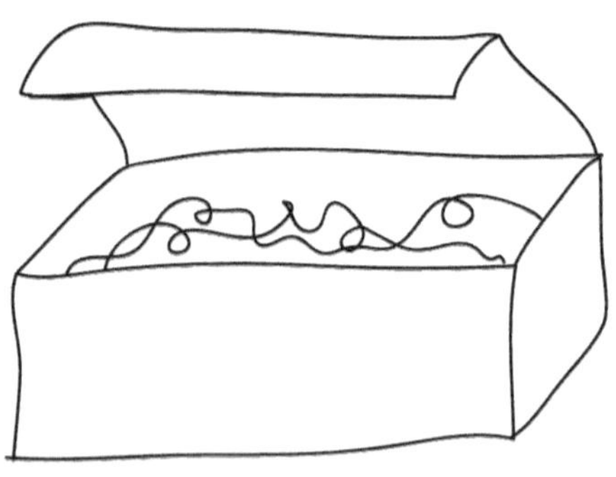

I am a mouse
I don't get angry
I just get scared
fear rules me
no other emotion
and the moment I let my guard down
and allow myself
any other emotion
happiness
contentment
peace
and trust the world
something grabs me
every time
telling me
to keep everything right and in balance
I must be scared
so everyone else can be happy

~ *amba elieff*

The trestle still lives
in my memory
that moment
rising high in the air
I can close my eyes
and see it
feel the fear and the courage
and the wind
pushing me from behind
as recklessness pulled me forward
afraid of heights
not afraid of death
afraid of falling
too young to be afraid of dying
and happy enough
to not welcome it

~ *amba elieff*

Deep inside me is a small box
it is padded
inside I have stuffed
hope
faith
belief
love
I try to lock it closed over and over
but it never works
I end up pushing my hand against it
shoving with all my might
again and again
so they can't get out
and hurt me

~ amba elieff

So many mirrors of perfection
you put before me
all my life
til
the mirrors were like a fun house
everywhere I turned
and looked
another distortion of me
another twist
fat, short, deformed
by the mirrors
by your eyes
til I could see nothing else

~ amba elieff

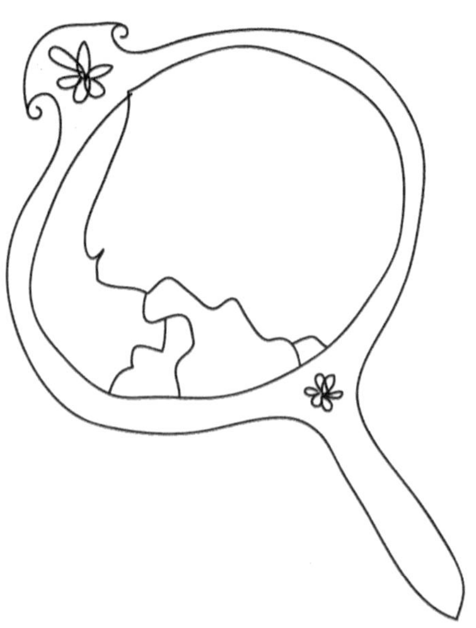

It is always the scent
that stops me in my tracks
and starts my head spinning
and stops my heart
and I hold my breath
wondering where it is coming from
what does it mean
it smells like her
a deer in headlights
I want to run
I am frozen
the scent
brings me back to
doubt and questioning everything
and the story that
I was trying to believe

- *amba elieff*

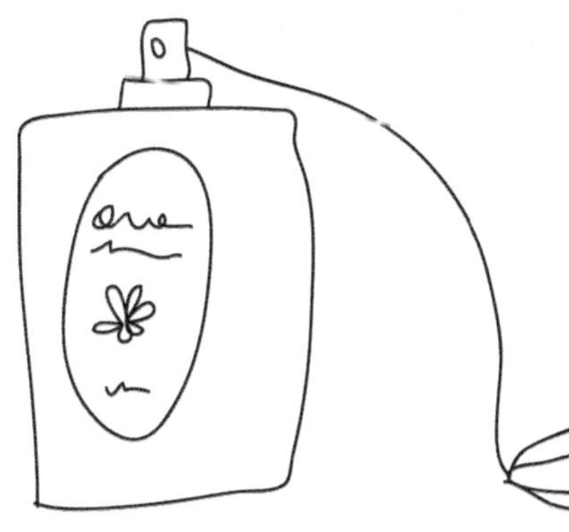

I was young
and forbidden
that made me
more tantalizing
more of a catch
something to flaunt
and I was young
and naïve
to think
the gleam in his eye
was love
and not conquest

~ *amba elieff*

Online
incessantly
because it gives me something to look forward to
one thing that will happen sometime in the future
that is not a surprise
I get to feel anticipation
I have something that I can get excited about
I get to feel something that is not sad and worry
and fear
The UPS man
The FedEx man
The Mailman
carrying a box or bag
that has the goodies inside
the bag or box that gave me something to look
forward to
a future – something in my future
even if it is only a week long future
and the feelings of being eager for something,
excited, anticipation
One thing for me to look forward to

~ *amba elieff*

I had a crush on you
and you
and you
all of you
that noticed me
that were simply nice to me
I needed someone to value me
see worth in me
so anyone that made me feel appreciated
a little interesting
I fell for
hoping that someone
might have a crush on me

~ *amba elieff*

You showed up in my mind again
snuck in when
I wasn't paying attention
I think it was the scent
that made me feel
the shadow of you
behind me
wrapping your arms around me
the warmth of your breath
I closed my eyes
and
shouted
GET OUT.

~ *amba elieff*

This morning
drying my hair
watching the water drain
slowly
I feel the dryer in my hand
watch the water
enough to cover
the hairdryer
and then I could reach in
but
today is not the day

~ *amba elieff*

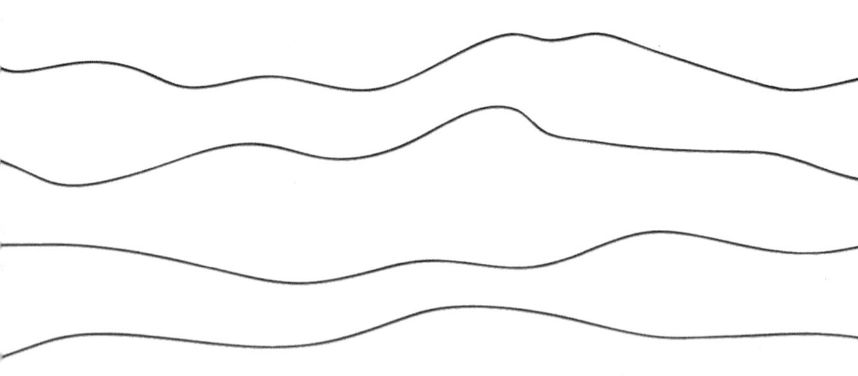

Watch him with others
the loud voice that makes you cringe
argumentative
black and white
belligerent
opinionated
never wrong
controlling
but he is not that way with me
give him time
you will get your turn

~ amba elieff

The first one
that called
and stopped by the house
that you lied to and told him
I wasn't home
I wasn't available
and you lied by omission to me
not telling me that he called
that he stopped by
the one that I loved
that was the good one
the others
they were all monsters

~ *amba elieff*

In these pages
you will find
madness
and
by exposing
the madness
we heal

~ *amba elieff*

I need a new beginning
a place to start over
where I can feel safe
find trust
find myself
I've been so lost for so long
a new beginning
a fresh start
I close my eyes and try to see it
a spiral that ascends to a new place
higher ground
a beginning
a fresh start
and

I see a spiral that looks like the same
the same feelings
same fear
same distrust
same path
so I open my eyes

and trudge ahead one more day

~ *amba elieff*

My mind
it asks questions
I am afraid to have answered
but I need the answers
but if the answers aren't the ones that I
want and need
I know I will crash
emotions overwhelming, thoughts endless

Right now I am treading water
I can do that a long time
not knowing
wondering
as I tread water
waiting for the answer to surface
like a leaf floating on the water
the answer always comes eventually

And if I crash
I will continue
and return to
treading water again

~ *amba elieff*

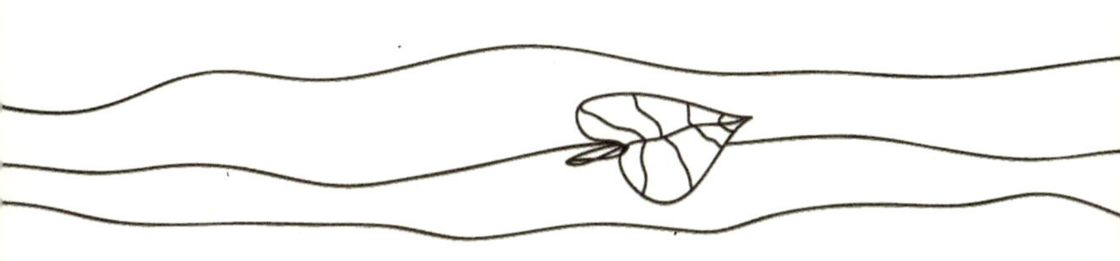

You
are like a splinter
under the skin
I can never get all of it
it breaks
and works its way deeper
til
it feels like it is gone
then it comes back
through the layers
to the surface
of the skin
one more time

~ *amba elieff*

Boys
taught me early
say no
and they leave
being loved goes away
and I wanted to be loved

so
I traded my value
my worth
to be loved
to just say yes
accept the exchange

~ amba elieff

Some demons we are
born with
some we earn
by our decisions
and some are given to us
like presents
wrapped in a pretty package
just waiting

~ *amba elieff*

How long did you watch me
prey
unobserved
making conversation
planning what to say
gathering information
so you knew
how to play me
vulnerable
make me feel loved
make me feel wanted
make me feel like you needed me
not just my body
You set the hook deep
leaving
and returning
leaving
and returning
til I was scared of losing you
well played
prey caught

~ *amba elieff*

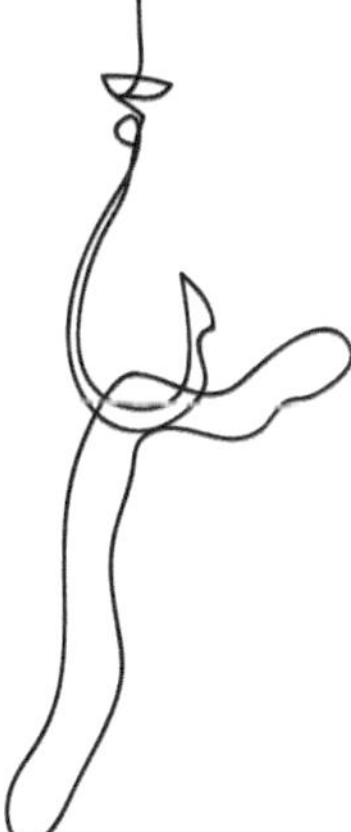

I am still the fool
so I stay
away from
everyone who knows
the truth
I couldn't see

so I feel
a little less foolish

~ *amba elieff*

The hills that I love
my peace and comfort
my future
my dream
sometimes I wonder
if you can see them
from your cell
through the bars
or is it only when
you are released
into the yard

~ *amba elieff*

Fierce and independent
in a college English class
the question
what do you think of terms of endearment
a class of mixed ages
at 21 I am young
surrounded by wisdom
I could not yet see
and the word
I am certain
I would never be called
because I found it demeaning
"babe"
I was going to be no one's babe
and
I look back at myself
from 20 years later
and grimace
but I let him call me "chick babe"
and I was proud
that is how he saw me
a chick and a babe
all my fierce, feminist, independence
shattered
it should have been a warning

~ *amba elieff*

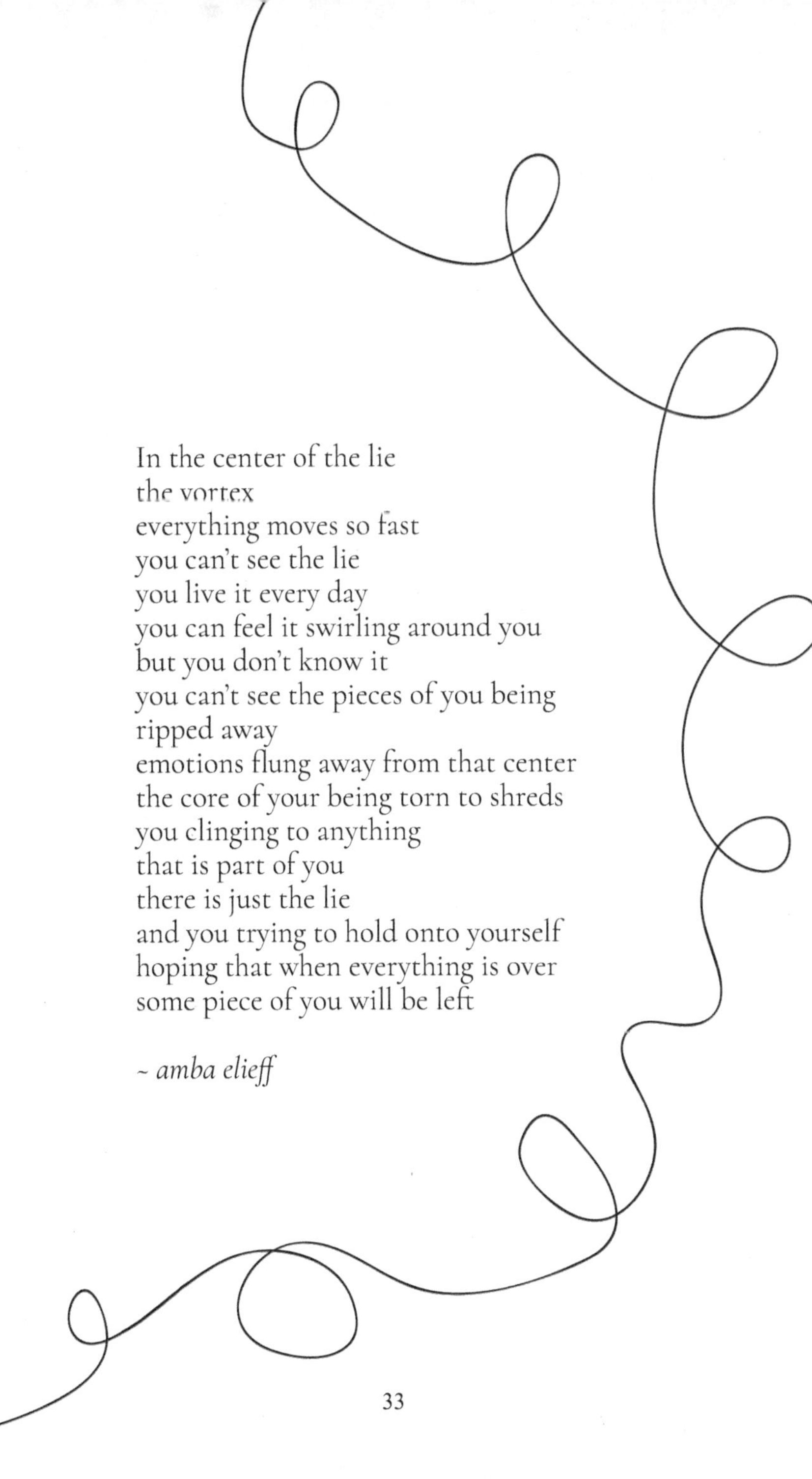

In the center of the lie
the vortex
everything moves so fast
you can't see the lie
you live it every day
you can feel it swirling around you
but you don't know it
you can't see the pieces of you being
ripped away
emotions flung away from that center
the core of your being torn to shreds
you clinging to anything
that is part of you
there is just the lie
and you trying to hold onto yourself
hoping that when everything is over
some piece of you will be left

~ *amba elieff*

Knowledge is power
but often
the truth, the knowledge
scares me

~ *amba elieff*

I wanted someone to give me a story
make me meaningful
I wanted to be important
to someone
I wanted to finally
feel loved
you saw it
the need
the emptiness
how lost I was
and you fed me a story
you knew exactly
how to craft it
and I devoured it
ravenous for someone
to want me
need me
love me
I thought it was beautiful
love and light
then the cracks started
slowly showing glimpses of darkness
til everything was
dark
and twisted
and completely dead inside
that is when everything became real

- *amba elieff*

Every time he left
I cried
he left a lot
what a waste of tears

~ *amba elieff*

I was blinded
by your words
and tears
flattered
by your attention
and you wrapped
all of it up into
promises
I was determined to believe
this time
I could not imagine
a reason
that you would not be true
honest
foolish
as I realize
all you left me with
was a label

mistress

~ *amba elieff*

Hurt a mother's child
and in an instant
she changes
she becomes someone
you never knew existed
a person on the edge
of crazy
and the lens she looks through
only sees her hurt child
and
she will do anything
to stop that hurt
the world becomes
a frightening place
everywhere she looks
there is danger
distrust
and
she will do most anything
to right the wrongs

~ *amba elieff*

Me
living life
naive
too busy
waiting and watching
for the happily ever after
to realize
I am not in a romance novel
it is a psychological thriller

~ *amba elieff*

Lies simply nudge
they are subtle
they are sneaky
they start the story
then you live with it
making it believable

~ *amba elieff*

When I was born
my parents gave me a box
inside was all the things
I could have in life
I was a girl
the box defined me
Wife
Mother
Homemaker
Teacher maybe
demure, quiet, pretty, congenial
this was who I was allowed to become
I took things out of that box
I tried them on
most of them didn't fit
I did become a mom
a mom who gave my girls a box
so big
they could do anything
be anything
be amazing
I just hope it was a big enough box

~ *amba elieff*

I was blinded
by your words
the pictures you painted
with them

you baptized
your promises
with your tears
so real
I believed them

the tears
and the promises
and the words

young and foolish and alone
I could not see the truth

~ amba elieff

Please do not make promises
you won't keep
because
then
I will have to leave

~ *amba elieff*

I don't care if you
lie to me
just don't ever let me
find out

~ *amba elieff*

Baby
thrust into the world
no longer floating
in a soft, warm place
but now a place
with hot and cold
and things have edges
and there is hunger
and we hope in our tiny bodies
to feel safe and loved
that we will be fed
kept warm
comforted
but we are helpless
with only a cry
that can crescendo into a wail
for someone, something to take care of us
I search my memory
watching myself age
I don't remember
those feelings
safe and loved

~ *amba elieff*

Where do I live
in the story
I choose to believe
pretend
or
in the truth
with a world
that is unknown

~ *amba elieff*

Life is chaos
food can be controlled
if I control food
I control life
five saltines
lots of tea
some honey
an apple
that is enough
a day done
life controlled

- *amba elieff*

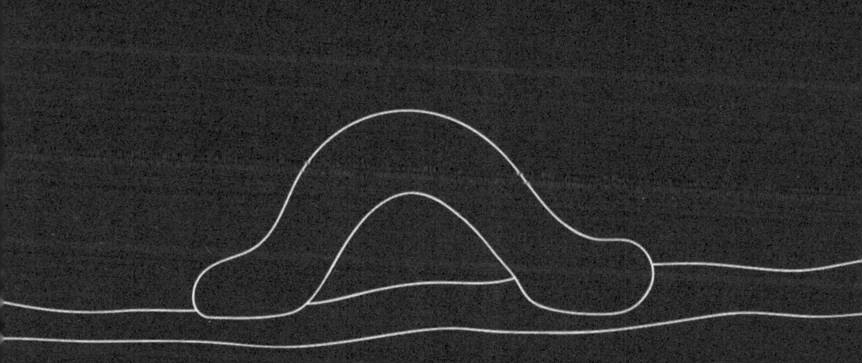

FALL EQUINOX

The days are equal dark and light. A time of transformation moving toward winter. A time of realizations.

And in a moment
we go back to the beginning
back to the wondering
back to the doubt
because
once
I trusted so easily
and so much
and forgave
until all that was soft
and believing
got edges
everything covered in suspicion
time
time lets the edges soften again
let down the guard
but if you slip ever so little
I regret
and edges get tough and stiff and hard again
and we are back at the beginning

- *amba elieff*

Relationships
joining my life with another
creates struggle
requires compromise
requires trust
trying to find peace
with your history
with my history
to join those lives
make them work as one
make them a single life
instead of two
it requires belief
it requires honesty
we have to talk to find the peace
in that life
will I be able to talk
can I find that peace

~ *amba elieff*

Trained
from a young age
through relationships
people
something nice
means
someone is hiding something
they broke
they lied

Nice
makes up for
the thing
they shouldn't have done
that you might find out about
ease their conscious
ease the consequences
and I am left wondering
What?
What did you do?

~ *amba elieff*

I am up with the dogs
early morning stillness
early morning quiet
then there is the click
another Click
I have pulled out a photo album
I page through
the stillness and quiet are broken by the
clicks
and I pull out the photos
like pulling out an earthworm from its hole
in the rain

The photos encapsulated there
in the album
untouched
for years
this one is from before the secrets
this is from when we were all being
groomed
lured to trust, but I couldn't know that then

The photos stick to the PVC free plastic
like the worm clings to the hole
when you pull
to grab it and put it in the bucket
I have a small pile now
Click, Click, Click
your face. I hate it

~ amba elieff

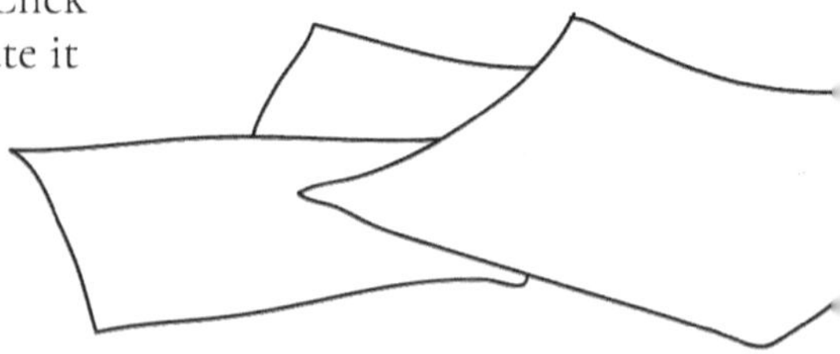

I leave some of the photos if it isn't your face
if there is something else that has value
I take the pile
put them in the trash
no dramatic rips or tears or burning
you don't deserve that much emotion or attention

Another moment
memory edited
so many more to go

The photo album has a new section
that is gap toothed
the white paper glaring
where vacations
birthdays
hikes
silly moments used to be
the next edit will be
to move the remaining photos
fill in the gap tooth spots
so that only the new edited memory will remain
and I won't miss or notice
the holes

- *amba elieff*

I can't watch you leave
I know it sounds silly
you aren't really leaving
it is a weekend
away
and you will be back
and your stuff is in the living room
ready to go
but I can't be here
when you leave
I watched too many times
others
pack and leave
return and leave
return
and leave again and again and again
a roller coaster of emotions
and each time someone leaves
it feels like I am getting back on that ride

~ *amba elieff*

There are pieces of me
so broken
that all my strength
holds them together
binding them tight
trying to make the seams disappear
so the feelings quit oozing out
making me weak

- *amba elieff*

You visited your other life
for a weekend
what life was before
me
kids, friends, activities
busy
as before
never home
and I wonder
did you really miss me

~ *amba elieff*

Sometimes
I look at your eyes
searching your face
trying to see what is real
and I can't
I can't find it
I can't discern anything
Is there nothing really there?
Is it all true?
or are you that smooth
my eyes roaming your face
I think
one day
I may have to leave
then there won't be anything
to search for

~ *amba elieff*

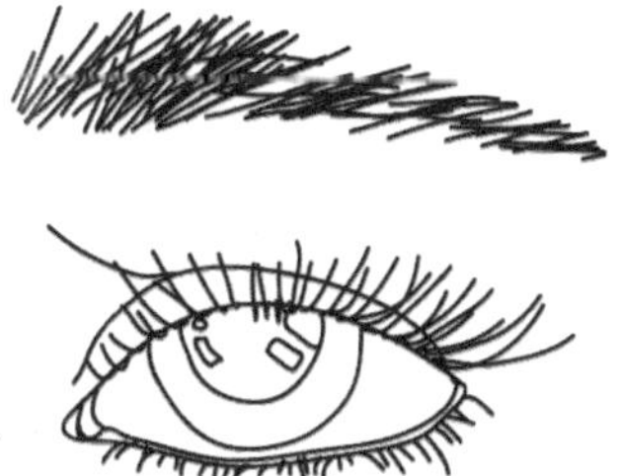

I am your storyteller
you never knew
all the stories my mind created
for you
excuses
to make living easier
to stay
looking for complicated answers
rather than acknowledging the simple truth
unable to say a word
to give the truth or lie a voice
knowing how the knowledge
would make me crumble
so I add another chapter

~ *amba elieff*

Trust is like a dream
lulling you
so everything is believable
and life feels perfect
and you accept everything
if the fact doesn't match
the trust
then you search for
plausible answers
the trust isn't broken
the world is
and when no answers match
the nightmare begins

~ *amba elieff*

Someone knew
I am certain of it
they saw the trap
the prey
they knew what would happen
if I stayed
they said nothing
but a prayer
of gratitude
their children were safe

~ *amba elieff*

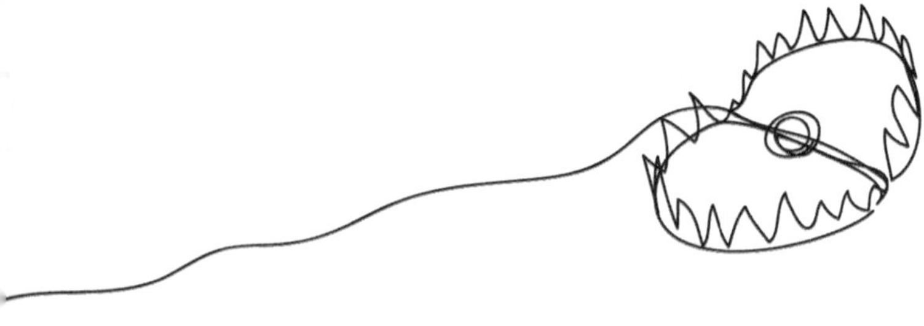

They read my diary
something sacred
I never imagined
they would
read my thoughts
my words

they threw
my
feelings
thoughts
actions
words
in my face
and I was never the same
the naive trust I had
destroyed
for everyone

~ *amba elieff*

Trauma
missing memories
gaps

a conversation
and one surfaces
a blank space
what do I choose
to fill it with

~ *amba elieff*

I look in the mirror
in the bathroom
in the bedroom
in the car
in the reflection of the window
and I wish I could see
all the words that everyone else sees
magical, lovely, beautiful, strong, intelligent, confident...
instead I see a woman who is alone, struggling to find herself
still uncomfortable in her own skin, worn looking, aged,
searching for some type of magic

~ *amba elieff*

I was the picture taker
I took all the photos
defined the history of my children

capturing what I wanted them to remember
what I thought was important
always behind the camera
never with them
photos of
birthdays, holidays, vacations
hanging at the house
pictures with the people
I thought were important
we would want to remember
I was so wrong
I captured a story
that was
a lie

~ *amba elieff*

You stole my love
my trust
my sanity
my heart
my memory
my story
you wove a tapestry so tight with
all of me intermingled with all of you
and now
all I can do is pull my threads forward
threads of me alone
til you are just a shadow in the weave

~ *amba elieff*

The demons
in my head
formless
noisy
are more terrifying
than the quiet monsters
that lived under my bed
when I was a child

- *amba elieff*

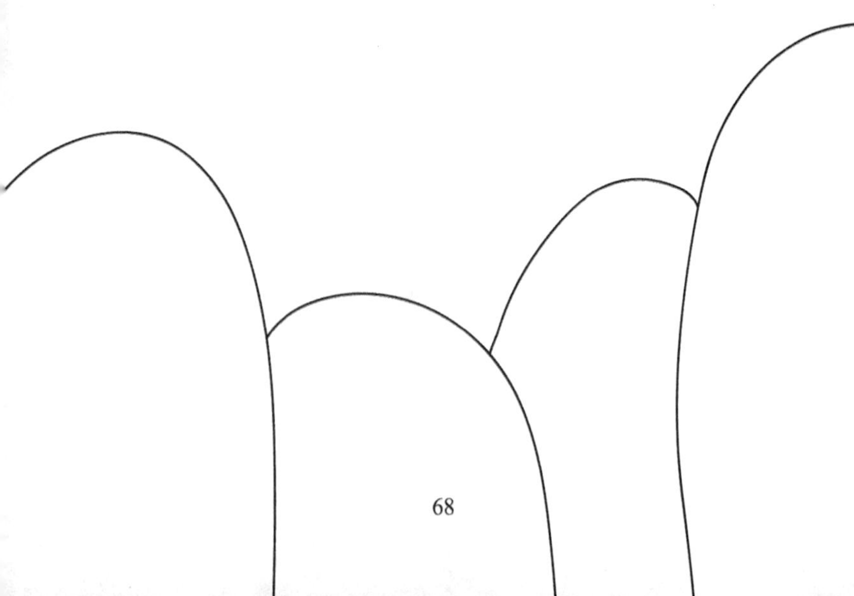

Self-esteem
No
Self-worth
Nope
gratitude
that you noticed me
are talking to me
and I will get
played again

~ *amba elieff*

Sometimes you still grab my heart
and take my breath away
just like the first time I saw you
just like the first time you held me
just like the first time you kissed me
just like the first time
I heard that you were a monster
and my heart squeezes tight
and instead of butterflies
now
my stomach is full of lead
and everything that was light is dark and heavy

~ *amba elieff*

I don't take pictures of people anymore
I used to be the one
capturing everyone's moment
pictures of my kids
birthdays
slumber parties
friends
events
family

And then I realized
people sometimes need erased
they are false
they are lies
they need edited out
the pictures trap you in a life
that exists forever
with those people
people you need to forget
memories you want to shed
and the pictures are a trap
where you are caught
like a bug in amber

- *amba elieff*

It was the last one that did it
emotions scattered and dismantled
trust and distrust
moved into my bones
buried
a battle
that pulled them into the marrow
trust and distrust
deep where the blood is born
and they tainted it
distrust always winning
always leaving me unsure
anxious
off center
afraid

the tainted blood
made me so hot
feverish
trying to kill off
the last remnants
of trust I might ever have
mutated the blood cells
replicated
til even when I would bleed
it was distrust that flowed
from the wound

~ *amba elieff*

Poetry
words hung together
on a line
like
airing out
my dirty laundry
in public

~ *amba elieff*

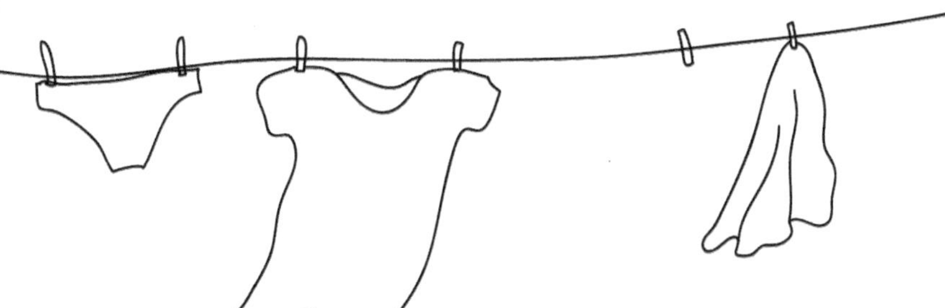

I trust you
right now
in this moment
us together
I can't imagine...

and I stop myself
because I can imagine
and I know
in the next hour
or two
or three
or a day
I won't trust you
I won't
and it cycles
between hours
or days
or weeks
everything perfect
and then a question
a suspicion
a fear
and I have to start over

~ *amba elieff*

The demons play
with your mind
and they spin you around
they twist stories
and thoughts
til you don't know
what is fact
what is fiction
then
they have you
you are filled with doubt
and you just silently cower
not knowing what to believe

~ *amba elieff*

I can't imagine anyone
actually loving me
I have no memory
of anyone being with me
for who I am
I am constantly cycling between whole and broken
I don't completely believe anyone
I get triggered
the fear constant like the alertness of a rabbit
I am not sure how much of this anyone sees
how visible it is
I am not sure if they know they can be hugging me
and I see my invisible arm holding
them away
at a safe distance
afraid of being hurt
afraid of being duped

~ *amba elieff*

Sometimes
trust
and
belief
just means
everyone else
got more clever
and devious

~ *amba elieff*

The truth will set you free
while everyone else
carries its weight

~ *amba elieff*

We went on vacation
gone a few days
took pictures
posted them
wrote a note
people liked
people commented
they saw the edited
happy
version
last night I checked my daughter into a
psych facility

~ *amba elieff*

And again
it is revealed
you are still
lying

unexpected
the truth

I am still
the fool
the butt of a joke
that is never ending
that is all yours

~ *amba elieff*

How do I start
the conversation
I don't know
so it never happens
just silence

~ *amba elieff*

I don't want to know
I could live in the lie
pretend everything was perfect

But I want to know
part of me always wants to know
then what would I do
retreat
leave
the best thing
because it wasn't perfect

~ amba elieff

I am still hiding
pieces of me
weighing
the risk of hurting them
instead of accepting hurting me

~ *amba elieff*

She could not silence herself
she had to warn everyone
tell the story
there was evil
and we had to protect the children
and
evil looked safe
and
safe was evil
and she was unable
to tell them apart
no one could tell them apart
and she couldn't protect
her children
Could anyone?

~ *amba elieff*

Thanksgiving
the prison parking lots are full
and I wonder
does anyone ever visit you
or did you disappear
for everyone else too

~ *amba elieff*

Dropping her off at school
early morning
middle school
kids everywhere
in groups and clumps
talking
goofing off
200 kids? 300?
and all I can see
is the statistic
1 in 10 will be
sexually abused
in childhood
and most will know
their abuser
I have to look away

~ *amba elieff*

Unspoken
I was never to ask questions
Unspoken
I was never to have an opinion
Unspoken
I was never to be loud
Unspoken
I was never to be discontent
Unspoken
I was not to talk about difficult things
and today
I am still
Unspoken

~ *amba elieff*

Slapped by the truth
when it reveals the lie
one moment life feels perfect
the next you know it is not

Left questioning
do I want to return
to just believing
the lie

Feeling the contentment drain
filled with emptiness
in the pit of your stomach
raw nerves
understanding
you can't go back

~ *amba elieff*

I will always remember
the card
first anniversary
you wrote
"You left footprints on my heart"
I should have trampled it
your heart
instead of letting you rip mine out

~ *amba elieff*

I thought I had finally
been blessed
with a love story
a dream come true
sometimes struggles
there are always struggles
but then I realized
it was all really
a nightmare

~ *amba elieff*

Relationships that should
be sweet
laced with trauma
like arsenic
on powdered sugar donuts

~ *amba elieff*

We have 10 years
the two of us
still
loosely tied
in 10 years I get to move
retire
to the cabin
the place I love
the place that kept me alive
allowed me to survive
all the dark
you created

and you
will be released
into the world
no more bars
and orange jumpsuits
return to what life is left
for you
I pray you will leave
the place that I love
because they locked you up there
your 20 years
of seeing my hills are over

mine will just be beginning

irony

- amba elieff

For him there is a
"one who got away"
I have heard about her
they dated til long distance ended it
I know her
I still see her
and she is beautiful
a good mom and wife
and always looks happy
and I stop and wonder
Is that your happy that got away?

~ *amba elieff*

In love
she could only see
a forever
a happily ever after
sacrifice
torment
secrets
tears
misery
anguish
joy
euphoria
stop
you aren't in a romance novel
these are red flags
this is reality

~ *amba elieff*

Marriage
filled with
a single mantra
I agree to disagree
I agree to disagree
everything he said
I responded
I agree to disagree
there was no middle ground
there was no gray area for him
and tired
of repeating
that same line
I became silent
and I finally
became strong
and
walked away

~ *amba elieff*

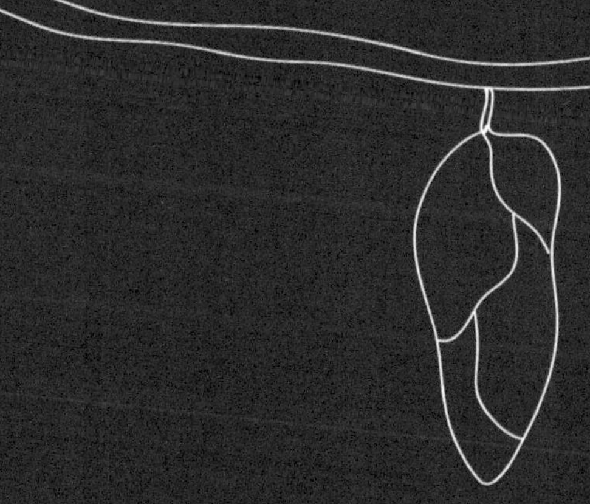

WINTER SOLSTICE

The longest night of the year. A dark time hoping to survive the night to begin another year. This is a dark place. Depression and the weight of life can be so heavy during this time of year.

There was a darkness
that descended
on everything
and everyone
the world
became a scary
place
full of people
wanting to hurt you
and
people
wanting to love you
but you could no longer
tell them apart

- *amba elieff*

I lay here and hold him tight
I love him
I breath him in and snuggle close
and the entire time
all I can think
is that I can't imagine him loving me
he says he does
he holds me close
I know that he wouldn't be here if he didn't
but I can't fathom
why anyone would love a human as flawed as me
anyone loving me
anything about me that would make
someone love me and stay

~ *amba elieff*

Defeated
end of the day
long day of ups and downs
of sore hands
tired mind
and then big things that were
supposed to be taken care of
no worries
still there undone
and I want to cry
and I catch the smell of her
on your shirt
and I am completely defeated

~ *amba elieff*

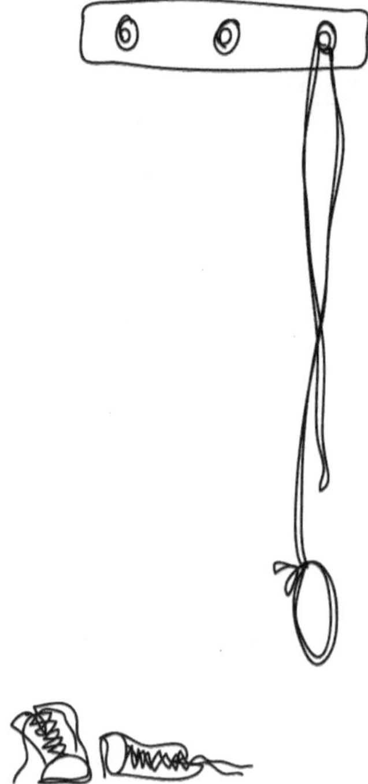

There are lots of lost days
days where I wait
days where I pace
days where I sit and read
and pace
and wait
and accomplish nothing
but I can't leave
I am trapped
by what ifs
and by fear
and by this lump in my stomach
that paralyzes me from leaving
and I pace
and I wait
and I think I might take a walk
I think walking the dog would be a good idea
but something
that is in me
that I feel
makes it hard
to leave
and I pace some more
until the entire day is lost

- amba elieff

I can't forgive
there are too many night terrors
remembering therapy appointments and medica-
tions – depression, anxiety, sleep
too many thoughts that run through my mind that
I can't stop
I can't get rid of
memories of you that are twisted like a car
wrapped around a tree
mangled and tangled and burnt out
my body feels like it was thrown
broken and bruised by the memories

I can't forgive
everyday watching her struggle
not just sometimes
struggle with the nightmares, night terrors,
sleepless nights, afraid to go to sleep
exhausted mornings that run into exhausted
afternoons
trying to catch some peaceful sleep that often
won't come
then homework that piles because exhaustion is
too much for a classroom
exhaustion is too much for concentration
and the flashbacks
and the stares that go to some other place and time

I can't forgive
there is too much worry
medications locked in boxes
knives locked away too

I carry the keys everywhere
fear that when she wakes her mind will not be in a
good place
fear that if I leave something will happen
worry that something will remind her
and she will hide in the closet
and she will be trapped writing as her only
communication
because the silence you created was so long and
deep
speech will not come

I can't forgive
though I have been told it will give me peace
that it is necessary to move on
that I must so I can heal
but all of them are not here
where I live, every day... waiting, worrying, afraid
I can't forgive

~ *amba elieff*

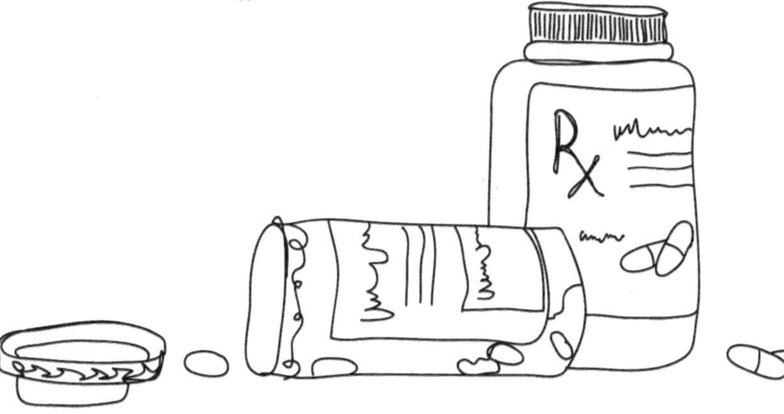

It is the long lies
that cause the damage
small lies
that live a short moment
and pass
float away
like dandelion seeds

But the long arduous lies
bury themselves like a tick
sucking your soul
and bleeding you dry
til there is very little left

~ *amba elieff*

I was still so young
I didn't know
I didn't understand
how powerful words are
how they can trap you
and I told him
I belong to you
and I thought
I belong to you
and I thought
you belong to me
and those words
I can't get back
and those thoughts are there forever
and I don't belong to him
and I don't belong to me
caught in past moments
I can't retrieve me
and
belong to anyone else

~ *amba elieff*

There are so many nights
that I do not sleep
I lay in bed
and I float
my body relaxes, eyes close, and my mind wanders
aware of everything
the press of the dog against my side
each shift and sigh he makes
each move my husband makes shifting, snoring
the soft snores of the tiny dog
at the foot of the bed
sound asleep
all of them
as I float
not awake
not asleep
some place safe
where I can't be hurt or surprised
aware but unaware
til morning

~ *amba elieff*

So, what does depression look like
everyday working 12 hours a day to keep busy
on a Saturday reading a 400-page book
not leaving the house
yelling at the dogs
eating ice cream for dinner
wondering if there is a yoga pose for depression
and going back to that 400-page book because
it takes you someplace other than here

~ *amba elieff*

Day - by day, by day, by day, by day, by day, by day
broken up by hour after hour after hour after hour
filled with the silence minute by minute by minute
by minute
like a waiting room
silent screams in my head
each second
and I sit consuming the words in the stories
in the books, all the books
so the screams will be silenced
and I will go someplace else
with other people that don't exist
but do exist in the stories
and time will pass
hour after hour after hour after hour
minute by minute by minute by minute
day by day by day by day

~ amba elieff

The blank stare, and the eyes looking upward
forward, into nothing
Are you okay?
I don't know
Can I get you something?
I don't know
Can you tell me what you are thinking?
I don't know
Do you want to go to the barn, the store, the
kitchen, the...?
I don't know
Do you want something to eat?
I don't know
the stare is constant

Looking at that thing I cannot see
I am not sure that she can see it either
sometimes I think she is just looking for it
whatever it is
Are you safe?
I don't know
and I don't know either

- *amba elieff*

I let my memory wander
to the warm spot you always kept for me
and the arms that encircled me safe
I felt so loved
so protected
so nurtured
so much trust
I miss that
those are the memories that make me cry
because you gave all of that to me
all of that I never had
such wonderful gifts
then you destroyed it so completely
small pieces that I can't ever put back together
you gave me gifts and destroyed me with them
now I can't have any of those things
I so desperately wanted

- *amba elieff*

There is a rhythm
in the poetry
I write
a heart beat
of the people
I have been
and the one
I hope to become
all of them
alive in me
somewhere

~ *amba elieff*

The milk is almost gone
the list is on the table
Bread, Eggs, Butter, Milk
the child is in the bed
blankets over her
staring
at nothing
at everything
indifference owns her
I cannot leave
I don't know what she might do
the knives are locked away
so are the pills
but I must stay
I cannot trust to even get the milk
or take care of the list
I am trapped

~ *amba elieff*

Please don't break promises
don't give me regrets
disappointments
don't lie
trust, belief, faith
has been broken
and repaired
so many times
I don't know
what I would come back like
if I had to do it again

- *amba elieff*

Somewhere there is a shoe box for my soul
simple and cardboard
a place to put me in when I die
where it is quiet
nothing in or out
just dark
silence
No demands
No wishes
No wants
No hopes
No fears
No expectations
put me someplace
and let my soul finally rest

~ amba elieff

Demons
still define me
define my needs

these are simply
the things I search for
the things I need
to fill in the holes
and feel complete
I need to be touched
feel your hands on my skin
hugged like you mean it
tell me you love me
til it is branded on my soul
and hold me
long after I feel safe and secure
give me promises I can believe in
so I never need to question
why you are here

~ *amba elieff*

Face value
in another life
I took everyone
at face value
I believed they showed
their true selves
so naive
and
he was kind
considerate, thoughtful
holding an invisible mirror
to me
reflecting back
a story like my own
unhappy marriage
adores kids
loyal and faithful
unhappy
stays in his marriage because of the children
and then he met me
and his life changed
and I was all he could think about
and I was starved for attention
could not see
that I was entering a romance novel plot
where I wanted him to be happy
and save him
give him the life he wanted
when all he wanted
would destroy everything he touched
that was precious to me

~ amba elieff

Tears fall from my eyes
poems flow from my fingers
and my voice
is a silent scream

~ *amba elieff*

I was transparent
a ghost girl
each person
took their box of pencils
and colored me in
to be what they wanted
when they were done
they simply erased me away

~ *amba elieff*

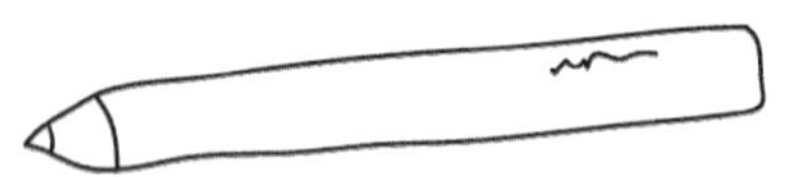

You are there
unspoken
in every memory
every story
a shadow
I can't escape
a lie of omission
as I say "the girls and I"
I can taste the lie
it is bitter
because you were always there
never was there
a girls and I
until you were gone

~ *amba elieff*

I woke to a blanket of snow
snow that normally cleansed me and everything
made the world feel new

Not this time
the snow lays heavy on my soul
a weight I could not ignore
that pushed me down
made me feel alone
in the quiet
no longer alive
not filled with the wonder of it
like sitting next to death
Waiting...

- *amba elieff*

I gave him too much of me
I opened myself up
and let him into
all the nooks and crannies
I made myself
soft
open
and he left
me hard
wary
and
disassociated
life no longer
to be lived
simply to be survived

~ *amba elieff*

Walking in and out of your life
that is what people do
sometimes intentional
sometimes not
the first time
devastated me
and over time
each time
someone walked away
searing pain
til now
when it doesn't matter
you can just walk away

~ *amba elieff*

Food
breakfast
I allow myself
a glass of milk
later in the day
the hunger pangs start
and I am hungry
but nothing sounds good
I turn off that part of my mind
and I am stronger than
the hunger
if I ignore it
it will go away
and it does
everything is good
til my body can't get warm
no food
no calories
no heat
and I can't get warm
I layer
and I crawl under a blanket
feeling my insides shiver
I drift off to sleep
no hunger there

~ *amba elieff*

Another day
they are all the same
endless
survival
getting cleaned up
ready for work
standing in the bathroom
drying my hair
watching the water
in the bathtub
slowly drain
it is clogged again
and
I have the thought
drop the hairdryer
splash into the water
reach in
and grab it
none of it will matter anymore

~ *amba elieff*

Boundaries
I set them up all around
then I quietly wait
til that moment
when someone reaches out
and touches one
like a trap unhinged
and everything stops
frozen
hiding
waiting
hoping everything will go away

~ *amba elieff*

It is the shock
and the crystal clarity
of the picture in my mind
of his face
staring up at me
his liquid brown eyes
so full of trust
that spoke volumes
in his silence
not understanding
that I would walk away
and never see my little boy again
trusting someone would love him
take care of him better than me
and I carry the heaviness
of never knowing
if that is true
or if the eyes
are still searching
each face
for me

~ *amba elieff*

There is a balance
between life and death
life can be terrifying
death can be terrifying
if she can just keep
death more terrifying
than life

~ *amba elieff*

Somedays you still consume me
I no longer feel the touch
that haunted me
this is deep inside
where you twisted all the emotions
made it so my trust was so broken
no one else could ever have me
I would never be able to believe or trust
anyone again
and in that simple reality
I would always be yours
you would always have me

~ *amba elieff*

Somewhere in the snow
I left the pieces of me
that were struggling to survive
hope, belief, faith, trust
each one broke off
like frozen icicles
falling jagged into the snow
leaving four pierced places
the corners of a square
boundaries to outline
what was left in my soul
Nothing

~ *amba elieff*

Suicide is like smoking
once you have tried it
it is always there
always an option
it never goes away
stress in your head
emotions overwhelmed
and you go there
if everyone is lucky you
find your way back out

~ *amba elieff*

The snow gave me clarity
deep, white, cold
I lay there
and I see each of them
three relationships
three lives
I chased each of them
each mistake was a choice
the cold numbs my regret, sadness
everything
and I know
I would repeat each choice
there is no peace in some lives
we repeat rather than learn
so I will lay in the snow
and have it hold me
til everything goes away

~ *amba elieff*

Today I woke up to shadows
not really surprised
the darkness was
seeping in last night
the darkness is comfortable
the weight of it
safe
pressing everything else out
including the words
it is all silent
in the darkness
then the shadows come
they keep me tethered
to the earth
so I don't slip
in the rest of the way
into the darkness
and disappear

- *amba elieff*

The pills
they quieted my mind
and the poetry went away

~ *amba elieff*

Even now
I don't confront anyone
I don't accuse
I don't argue
I just let the knowledge
of the truth
seep
into my bones
through my pores
til I am heavy
with the truth
of the lie

~ *amba elieff*

I never knew a man
who didn't lie
some by omission
some with a story
some to me
some to others
but they all lied
I learned their lies
and
I am still watching
waiting
to find one
that does not

~ *amba elieff*

Each of us have
time missing
grief
anxiety
fear
the trauma
the medications
erased
days
months' worth
years' worth
memories one of us will share
and the other two
stare blankly
as if we didn't live
in the same house
yet we did
minds protecting us
from what was

~ *amba elieff*

There is dead space
in my mind
that should be filled with
color, smells, sounds
but instead
my mind keeps it empty
to protect me
from all the chaos
and damage
he caused

~ *amba elieff*

I never know
why the memories come
but they do
once in awhile
and they are so vivid
I can see his face
the brown green of his eyes
and I can't shake them
and then as I blink
I can see my baby's eyes
warm and brown
adoring and trusting
and I can't shake that either
and anxiety
builds
and I reach for the bottle
just one pill will settle it down
I hope
and if one doesn't
I will take another
and another

~ *amba elieff*

He would catch my face in his hands
held
still
so I couldn't turn away
so I couldn't avoid his lips
as they came down on mine
no longer a choice
for me
held still
til he decided
to let go

~ *amba elieff*

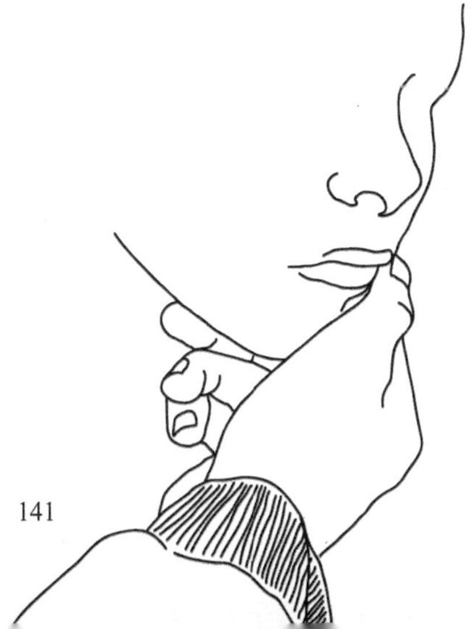

It is that time again
the cycle
when I want to quit
quit getting up
quit going to work
quit going nowhere
quit the stagnation
never going forward
without going backward
trapped in a place
where no one ever gets ahead
and I take a big breath
and I get up
and I go to work
and the cycle begins again

~ *amba elieff*

Life has taught me how to exist
in this place
you do not change
or grow
or thrive
you simply cling to routines
get up
go to work
go home
go to bed
and you repeat
and cling
til you can
move to a place of life

~ *amba elieff*

She thought he was home
safe and forever
only to realize
he was just
another place
to die

~ *amba elieff*

It took a very long time
for me to feel missed
I did not see myself
as being that special
to anyone
as having any worth
I imagined
if I disappeared
went away
it would have no meaning
life would go on
with one less chore
one less responsibility
there would barely be a hiccup

~ *amba elieff*

The falling snow lay heavy and wet on the hemlock
and pine
weighing the limbs pushing them toward the earth
the snow whispers to them, this is how she feels
when they don't listen
and leave her
rooted unable to move
trapped by something she can't see
invisible

The trees sighed
when the spring breezes come our limbs that feel
her pain
will lift and give her shelter beneath our boughs
she can crawl beneath and we will teach her how
those roots that hold us fast
tie us to the mother earth
to nurture us not trap us

She can roll in our soft needles and feel comfort
smell the love of the trees and earth
we will show her how to wave her arms like our
limbs in the wind and free herself
the wind in our boughs will whisper to her how
much she is loved

a part of all that is...

~ *amba elieff*

I quit everything
and my soul shriveled up
a raisin hard and wrinkled
with nothing to believe in
nothing to hope for
no longer a story
barely a footnote
and I moved through another day

~ *amba elieff*

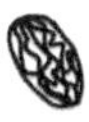

Relationships
I am an open book
I will tell you anything
and often I do
and then
regret
fear
What if they tell someone?
What if it comes back
to hurt me?
Would they?
and I retreat
never learning the lesson

~ amba elieff

The snow brought with it deep thoughts
How long do you want to live in the world
above the snow?
I want to live long enough to enjoy life
And how long is that?
I paused and thought
I counted
and I realized
it was too late
I could just sit and let the snow take me
now

- *amba elieff*

SPRING EQUINOX

The day is equal light and dark heading toward the summer solstice. There is a little hope here as we move toward the light of summer.

As long as I can remember
I wanted to belong
belong to a family
belong to a group of friends
belong somewhere
instead of disconnected
floating

Then I wanted to belong
to someone
romantic
soulmate
destiny
purpose
meaning
belonging to someone
and it failed

so now
although it's not much
I just belong to me

~ *amba elieff*

Erasing you
let's start in the kitchen
I got rid of
the tea pot
fondue set
wine glasses
cordial glasses
old bottles that were from you, sitting on shelves
reminders

Then the dining room
the napkins
placemats
a few knick-knacks
from you
we had to move the table
remove your chair
no place for you at our table

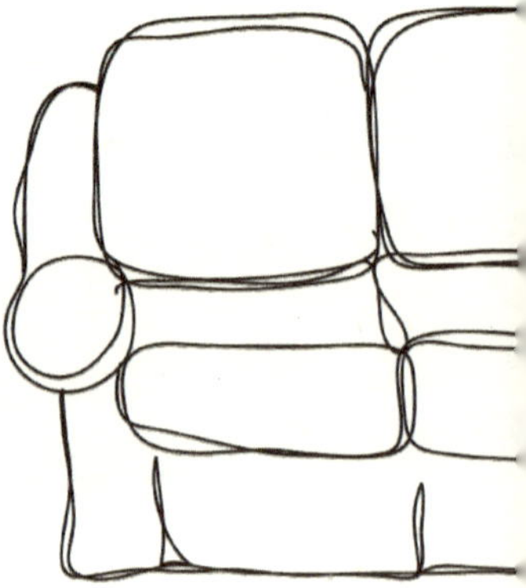

The living room
the couch
it still smelled like you
the chair
the pillows
memories scattered on tables
pictures of us
of you and the girls
all the framed prints
of old farmhouses something you once had and I
once wanted
the TV
the cabinet where the TV once lived
you watched the TV

We didn't
and we move everything
shift a little here a little there
just enough

The den
your desk
replaced with filing cabinets
no longer any memories from travels and day trips
no more pictures
you are gone

And then the bedrooms
the bed from my room
from my daughter's
her sheets and mine
her pillows and mine
all the mattresses
curtains
comforters
blankets
quilts
flannel shirts once yours given for comfort and
warmth
t-shirts once yours that I slept in
stuffed animals and souvenirs
the paint on the walls
more pictures
more knick-knacks and memories
drawers of cards and ticket stubs and letters emptied
furniture scrambled
it looks like my room now
my daughter will find her room one day too

~ *amba elieff*

I have a lifetime of hearing
the voice
in my head
if you do a job
you do it right
if you do a job
you finish it
I was never told
it was okay to fail a job
or better to try and fail
than not try at all

So I lived a lifetime
afraid to try
afraid I would fail
afraid I wouldn't be good enough
do the job well enough

So I spent a lot of my life
only trying when I knew
I could finish the job
and do it well
and do it right

What a waste of what I might have done

~ *amba elieff*

One picture of you
after hundreds I deleted
my penance
my albatross
a reminder of my stupidity
gullibility
one day when its found
I just hope
they understand
it isn't because I love you

~ *amba elieff*

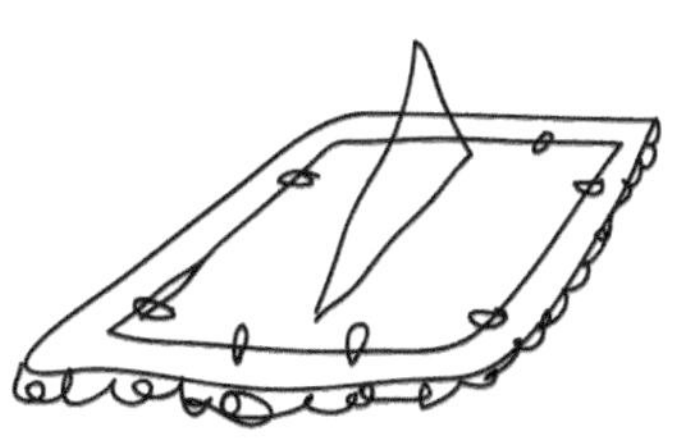

He gave me a story
something to believe
something to make me feel special
make me feel like we were destiny
but I had been told that story before
different but the same
and told another version
different but the same
and I so wanted to believe
and I can't imagine any story to be true
any story that involved being with me
so this time I walked away
grew

~ amba elieff

Sometimes my head hangs down
I will catch myself realizing the weight
and I am looking at the floor
it feels like you are hanging there
pulling me down
a weight around my neck
and it won't let go
I raise my head and it takes effort
it will try to drop again
and I stop it
I have no reason to hang my head
in shame
in embarrassment
one day this weight will be lifted
and you will need to carry it
because that is where it belongs

~ *amba elieff*

I promise I will try to trust you
it won't be easy
it will be work
it will be one day at a time
one moment at a time
it is hard to have something
you have never had
no one trusted me
from the time I can remember
I never saw what trust
looked like
felt like
and when I tried to trust
each time it was
shattered
not broken
not a piece chipped off
shattered
so now I will try to trust you
one moment, one day at a time

~ *amba elieff*

Another day
same earrings
they are silver
and dangle
a spiral etched in a circle
New Beginnings
this is what was written on the card that came
with them
I put them in every morning
a ritual, wish, habit, prayer
and in my mind I whisper
New beginnings
like a spell
like they contain magic
believing that I can trust through another day
of being with you

~ *amba elieff*

I am not alone
they are here
lurking in the corners
of my mind
you probably aren't alone
either
but we can both
domesticate our demons

~ *amba elieff*

I thought he broke me
and I had healed
I was back to one piece
whole
complete
then I realized
I was never broken
I was shattered
small pieces and jagged edges
scattered and hastily put together
with points
not smooth edges
not complete
small splinters missing
gone forever
so I can never be complete
I will always have pointed jagged parts
and splinters missing
and that will just be me

- *amba elieff*

My demons
all have names
I have lived with them
as long as I can remember
for a long time
they ran my life
filling me
with anxiety
always the rabbit
on edge ready to run
overthinking
everything
some of their names
distrust
doubt
self-worth
judgment
shame
depression
we live together
inside me
but now
sometimes
they listen to me

~ amba elieff

The poetry weeds
my mind
words phrases feelings
pulled out
like invasive plants
that do not belong
put onto paper
so flowers can grow

~ *amba elieff*

I kept one picture of you
from early in our relationship
in a frame
in a drawer
upside down
so I don't have to see it
I know it is there
reminding me
that evil resides
in the most loving of faces

~ *amba elieff*

I went to bed exhausted
so tired my body felt numb, heavy
I lay there
eyes closed trying to go to sleep
but the sounds outside my being
dishes, putting the dogs to bed, house sounds
then the reading light and the pages turning
everything breathing
and the noise inside my being joined the chorus
voices in my head, thoughts, lists, what ifs, you should haves
so I got up

I went into the other room
pitch dark
silent like a tomb
under my favorite quilt, old, filled with love and life
alone
and I was left with the noise inside my being
which I quieted til I was left with
my mind repeating
Rest beloved (inhale) You are okay (exhale)

- *amba elieff*

I thought I lost my soul
I stepped away
from everything
hiking, yoga, reading
learning, writing
everything that was me
until one afternoon
alone
depressed
I was looking in my closet
and saw my yoga mat in the corner
my magic raft that kept me afloat
in the ocean of life
prevented me drowning
over and over
and there was my soul
wrapped up in my mat
patiently waiting

~ *amba elieff*

Standing in front of my Keurig this morning
waiting for it to warm up
I think of you
I think that you won't get Constant Comment tea
in the morning in prison
I think that you don't look good in Orange
I think that you won't get salmon or steak or lamb
or lobster
I think that you won't be able to wear your hiking
boots
I think that all the food may just look the same
I think that there won't be fresh fruits or
vegetables
I remember how much you loved good food,
morning tea, comforts
I think that there won't be comforts anymore
and I am glad

~ *amba elieff*

I slipped backward tonight
sometimes it happens
when I least expect it
and you are there
and the thought is warm
and then the memory is before me
and then I feel cold
and confused
and sad
and I rip myself back into the present
where I can try to be safe again

~ *amba elieff*

My mind is still now
and quiet
no white pills
I found the one
who can wait
until I can put words
and a voice
to my doubts
patient and calm
I can ask the questions
and he answers
no need to fear
no need to worry
the story was all in my mind
life is much simpler
than the story in my mind

- *amba elieff*

Laundry
pile of clothes
checking pockets
dreading reaching into each one
things I might find
and there it is
another note
he is always so careless
I see her handwriting
no need to read it
I drop the pants
they fall on the pile
done
slip off my silicone ring
cut it in two
leave it on the kitchen counter
and walk out the door

~ *amba elieff*

Never be dependent on a man
emotional
or
financial
or
physical
Be safe

~ *amba elieff*

Still keeping secrets
omissions
edits
to my life
til the last one dies
then
Will I be free?

~ *amba elieff*

Ask the question
the worst
they can do
is say NO
and then you know
and move on

~ *amba elieff*

You don't belong here
in my mind
and heart anymore
I have given all
your places
to someone else
who will actually
take care of them

~ *amba elieff*

Each day I give you a piece of me
you don't realize it
I can't trust you with my whole being
I want to
but I can't
it isn't safe
but each day you get another piece
and you get closer
and I feel my body relax
a little more
a little softer
on the inside
where all the hurts are kept

~ *amba elieff*

I wanted to be
swept off my feet
by someone who was
madly and foolishly
in love with me
and each time
I got lost
in the abyss
hurt
struggling to reclaim
myself again

~ *amba elieff*

I was frozen in time
I did not know it
I thought I was living
one foot in front of the other
but I was merely
existing
waiting for an end
that would not come
I did not understand
I did not need an end
I needed a beginning

~ *amba elieff*

I will keep my mouth shut
But
My pen will never be still

~ *amba elieff*

Each day you get
a piece, a shard, a fragment
of me
I watch you try to put them together
they don't always fit
they don't always make sense
not even to me
all broken
pieces from a different version of me
but you puzzle each piece
til you find a way to make it fit
make me whole

~ *amba elieff*

Every time I look back
and wander into a memory
I tell myself
you were so young
and the foolish guilt and shame
that wells up
eases just a little

~ *amba elieff*

Change
takes
hours
days
months
years
but all you
remember
is
one day
everything was different

~ *amba elieff*

One day I looked in the mirror
and the face that looked back
was so different
for so long
I had kept my hair buzzed short
and my face was all
hard lines and tight muscles
looked like life
had sucked me dry
with my self-conscious
forced smile
it was safe that way
it kept people at a distance
but
he softened me
he told me I was beautiful
and he saw things I couldn't
then I let
my hair grow
and my face relaxed
and everything softened
and my smile became easy
and I started to see myself
as beautiful

~ amba elieff

There are no regrets
foolish things I did
brazen things I did
I do not regret
they are part of what has made me
who I am
but to speak of them
shame and embarrassment
creeps in
but
I am slowly
learning to let those go too

~ *amba elieff*

My world
is defined
by all the people
that were part of the story
a different life
that was a mistake
there was a full cast
friends, aunts, uncles, children, grandchildren
people I do not want to run into
so my world shrunk
there are cities that no longer exist for me
places I will no longer go
to ensure
I will not encounter
anyone
from that life

- *amba elieff*

She placed the babe in my arms
6 months old
a sack of potatoes
the baby reached for my necklaces
gumming the charms
bright eyes looking up at me
my body naturally
started swaying
the movement and rhythm
of a mother

I haven't touched a baby
in so long
10 years
15
so overwhelmed
for so long
only seeing
the evil that could happen to a babe
instead of the joy and hope they give away
holding her
everything was right in the world
and I got back
something he had taken away

- *amba elieff*

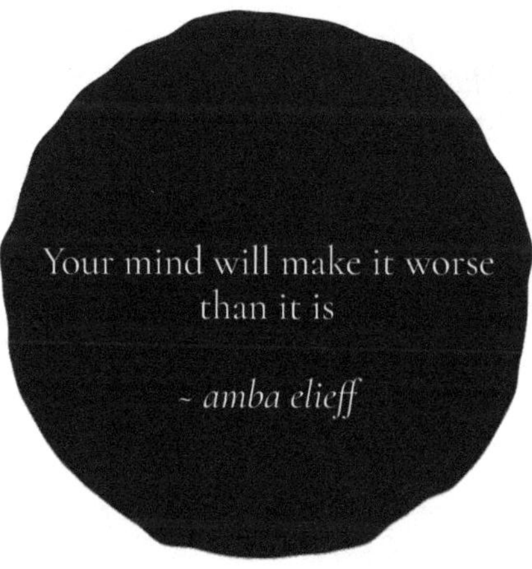
Your mind will make it worse
than it is
- amba elieff

It took me many years
to understand
that truth
is also a demon
for
it illuminates
the lies

~ *amba elieff*

My mind swirls
who do I believe
her story
his
mine
trying to sort it out
Why would she lie?
Is she remembering before?
Can he be trusted?
those moments I questioned
in my mind
and dismissed it
doubt
but there are no signs
the things I watch for
but still was I right
in wondering
does he do the things he does
to hide
or
to prevent
I still don't know
I have to make a decision
and I tell myself
I have to trust me
not her
not him
me
and keep moving
forward

~ *amba elieff*

Once I slayed my demons
and
you slayed your dragons
there was nothing left but magic

~ *amba elieff*

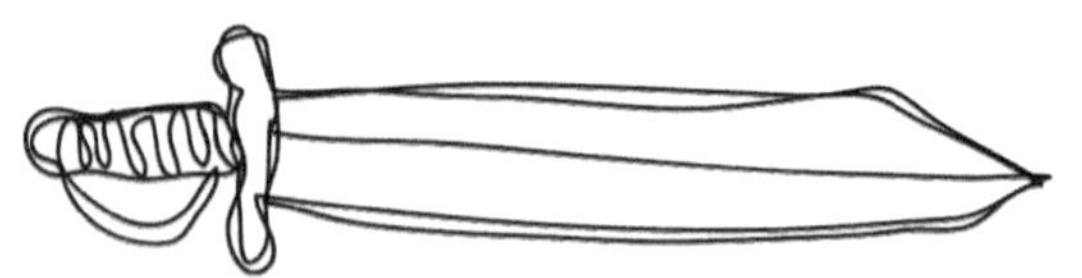

Sometimes I think
it took 5 years
for him to figure out
how to love me
then
I realize
it probably took
that long to slay his demons
too

~ *amba elieff*

The anger surprised her
angry was not an emotion
she ever felt
and this was like a tidal wave
crashing over her
she wanted to throw something
hear it crash
and break
where was it coming from
this surge
from deep inside her
suddenly
she realized
it was from the anxiety
the trapped feeling
the constant barrage of
words telling her she did nothing right
it was because
she finally knew what it was
to live without all that

the anger
was from being put
back in that cage

~ *amba elieff*

I wish
I were
a big bright beautiful
butterfly
stained glass wings
exquisite colors
floating and fluttering
amongst the flowers
in the sunshine
instead
I am a
moth
beating and battering myself
around the light
on a porch
in the dark

if you look closely
there is beauty
in that moth too
hidden colors
under my wings
as glorious, vibrant and mesmerizing
as any butterfly

~ *amba elieff*

PROMPT ME

This is a fun section in each of my volumes of poetry where I share poems that were created and inspired by poetry prompt challenges. The hardest thing for me with poetry prompts is following the rules (keeping to word limits) and picking the poem. Every prompt has so many poems hidden inside if you turn the words in your mind. Different viewpoints, different voices, endless possibilities. I hope you enjoy reading these as much as I enjoyed the challenge of writing them.

Poetry Prompt: Where lost souls go. This poetry prompt was from January 2022. It was a 48 hour poetry prompt with a word limit of 40. So many thoughts went through my head with this one. This is what I came up with.

I am
where lost souls go
hiking in the woods
reading a book
shopping online
working too much
eating a gallon of ice cream
hoping someone will find me
make me meaningful
help me find my soul

~ *amba elieff*

Poetry Prompt: Collection of skies. This was my first poetry prompt submission ever.

She looked in the mirror
both arms
mirror images
where he grabbed her
staring
she knows
the familiar collection of skies
her arms will become
Now dark gray, black and blue
stormy skies
angry, puffy
tinges of red
like the glow of a sunset
then
the lighter gray, dirty cotton
like summer rain clouds
then green like the skies
of a tornado
like his anger
blind
and finally
settling into the
melted butter yellow
like weak spring sunshine
hopeful
then healed
til his anger grabs her again

~ *amba elieff*

Poetry Prompt: Translucent thorn. This challenge was posted by a fellow poet online. She lives out west so a translucent thorn means something very different to her where there is no snow and ice. This was a week-long poetry prompt with no word limit. In an afternoon, I came up with this collection of poems.

A poem
translucent thorn
pondering words
phrases
massaging bodies
capturing words
well formed
segregating them
in my mind
trapping them
in order
massaging
remembering
scribbling them down
lines of the poem
the translucent thorn
finally gone

~ amba elieff

I worried it
that spot near my soul
the translucent thorn you left in me
buried
festering
no one can see
not even me
but I feel it
everyday
itching
painful
poking
til the poetry slips out
like puss on a page
and the itch stops
and the hurt lessens
and the day goes on
that thorn still pricking my soul

~ *amba elieff*

Translucent thorns
there were so many of them now
scattered
he sewed them well
deep in tissues
words of hate
derision
hits of anger
colorful bruises
around nerve endings
manipulation and control
constant fear
the spines go so deep
and even now
with him gone
the thorns press
and she can't escape
the pain

~ *amba elieff*

Succulents and cacti
lined on the sill
she strokes the succulent leaf
firm yet soft
pillowy
then her eyes turn to the cacti
prickly
breaks off a translucent thorn
rubs it carefully between her fingers
pushes it against the soft skin of her wrist
the small rush of pain
shock
she feels alive
the pain making her real
she pushes harder
wiggling it
til it disappears
under her skin
a constant pain
as she moves her hand
it pokes and buries deeper
reminder she is alive
she smiles
and snaps off another one

~ *amba elieff*

His hands glide
over my body
and his lips slowly tasted mine
then dipped between my breasts
his hand next to my heart
he paused
brushing the skin gently
tenderly
I realized he felt it
the translucent thorn
that I struggled with
always there
a prickly reminder
of all I wasn't
and he caressed it
til it disappeared

~ *amba elieff*

The storm over night
snow and ice
in bed I hear the ice pelting
pinging off the windows
tapping rhythms
frightening and soothing
dissonant
we wake to a wonderland
ice encapsulates everything
against a backdrop of white
the light from the sun blessing everything
branches shiny and slick with ice
pulled toward the earth
leaves trapped in clear amber
like a piece of art
and on the rose bush
translucent thorns
shimmer in the light
and we stare in awe of all the beauty

~ *amba elieff*

ABOUT THE AUTHOR

My name is Amba Elieff and I have been a closet poet my entire life. Writing poetry was my way of making sense of my world and emotions.

While I was writing poetry I was also experiencing life. I survived childhood and went to college. Got married and divorced. Had children. Had other relationships, some I probably shouldn't have. Worked for a "large corporation" most of my life only to have them lay me off at the age of 50 – so I went back to school and became a massage therapist and started over again. But this time starting over I had a wonderful husband who has always known I was a closet poet. And he also told me one day I would write a book. So I have started putting all those years of writing into volumes of poetry, and this is the beginning of my coming out of the closet.

I always imagined being published and now I am. I am Amba and I am a poet.

This is my second volume of poetry.

You can learn more about Amba Elieff, order copies of other volumes, and check out her merch, at her website, https://ambapoetry.com.

IG: @amba.elieff

ABOUT THE ILLUSTRATOR

When people ask Gabrielle Scarlett what she does for a living, she says that she "makes things pretty." She spends her work hours (and the personal ones, too) creating art in a variety of forms - from the physical kind that can hang on your wall, to websites and strategic brand suites for small business owners.

She now lives in Edinburgh, Scotland with her fiancé, but grew up in the same Ohio town as Amba, her mother. She too likes to think she's domesticated a variety of her demons, though admittedly via different means than Amba. Many of hers are tied to her disability - Ehlers-Danlos Syndrome - which she has spent her life learning to co-exist with.

You can learn more about Gabrielle on her website, https://gabriellescarlett.com.

IG: @thegabriellescarlett

www.ingramcontent.com/pod-product-compliance
Lightning Source LLC
LaVergne TN
LVHW091137080826
845145LV00008B/2179

9781968933067